skinless in the cereal aisle

Poems by

Scott Ferry

To Luke, man I
respect you so much!
I think you may get
this more than most.
Trudge through the
darkness, my friend!
—cheers!

ISBN: 978-1-914130-53-3

OTHER TITLES BY IMPSPIRED

Island –
By Clair Chilvers

Immersed in Blue –
By Margaret Royall

The Lane is a River –
By Ann Christine Tabaka

Old Wood Shop –
By Charlie Brice & Jim Hutt

Marty & Irene –
By Justin Wiggins

Beautiful Boy –
By Joseph Mykut

In Between Pauses –
By Amrita Valan

skinless in the cereal aisle – Scott Ferry

"I've been leaning towards the shadows all along"
-Townes Van Zandt

skinless in the cereal aisle – Scott Ferry

Acknowledgements

The following publications have included poems from this collection;

The Dope Fiend Daily: "dear scott"

Gyroscope Review: "i think i can create"

MacQueen's Quinterly: "otosclerosis and mandibular tori" and "when i cradle him god cradles me"

Meat For Tea: "i weep when i write" and "some days the restaurant of life"

Misfit: "shame dream 2"

Panoplyzine: "sometimes i wonder"

South Florida Poetry Journal: "awake at 4 am for no reason i think about"

The Rye Whiskey Review: "whiskey is horrible anti-anxiety medicine and why i don't drink anymore"

Verse-Virtual: "i will need to," "there are two worlds," and "what if"

Contents

Preface
By Scott Ferry

I was always a nervous kid. The anxiety that I have
walked around with from the beginning I assumed was
normal, that other people were just extremely brave or
had better coping mechanisms than me. While both of
those may be true, I still have recently realized that my
constant worry has clouded and scarred my jobs and
relationships much more than I have ever admitted to
myself. I spent every morning of my first (and horrible)
nursing job as a surgery nurse nauseated and every
weekend dreading when Monday would come. I thought
this would end when I quit this job, but it has resurfaced
every few years. I spent a large portion of the 2020-21
pandemic in this type of state. I first used alcohol and
exercise to manage the uptick of tension but soon that
was unfeasible because the alcohol would wear off and
leave me worse off, staring wide-eyed at three am into
some type of adrenaline void or other. So, I thought I
could talk myself and pray myself out of this cycle of
anxiety. In theory, it should be possible. No. I am
thankful that I reached out to my healthcare team for help
and for medicine. I don't wish this collection to be a self-
help gimmick, or an attempt to show how much I have
suffered. I just wanted to be real with the background
pain and static from which these poems were birthed. I

hope if you experience an ongoing mental health issue which you may not be admitting you have, that you do seek help. I know that, especially for men, society tells us that we shouldn't be weak and show our fear. And don't even get me started on this society's dismissal of the process of grief and healing. This book is a testament to survival through honesty to one's self and that help may be needed. I have found that it takes more courage to reach out for assistance as it does to live through self-inflected torture. I know my children and wife enjoy having me back in my body. Anyway, I hope you enjoy these poems. I appreciate your support!

shame dream

my clothes still off and my skin blistering
in front of the windows i see a line of people
i didn't notice before reflected in the periphery
and when i turn my head to focus on them
they turn into rosemary and lilac

they turn into statues of horses
i can't find my clothes and now my skin
is peeling off in continents and the bluebone
silk of my real skin glows when the dead layers
are wiped away

my penis is sapphire and my nipples are tangerine
and my hair is pearl and my fingers grow into vines
with winged flowers springing from the knuckles
the people are gone but i simmer in
coiled wait

when i wake i am ashamed i have shown too much
i am ashamed that my underskin surges out
like a swarm i am ashamed that these multipleasures
bound inside my pulses i am ashamed to appear
too much like a god

shame dream 2

why are these people in my bedroom
and when did i get a waterbed?
a neck-whistled gym teacher shouts *line up*
my sixth grade crush spins in chemin de fer jeans
my college roommate reads and never breathes
a blueskinned man vomits as i pull him out of the ocean
a sasquatch strings a violin and holds a poodle
my wife shoots her *how dare you* look from the hall
1974-era children climb the purple shoe
two dead friends young skin young skin
a jar of pickles open in my lap cold vinegar
my daughter repeats *dad you spilled*
dad you spilled my notebook wet
my pants soaked my son screams
because of the acid in his eyes he rubs them
with inky hands he rips the pages i had written
i had written our passwords our futures
my father laughs near the ceiling
my mother not yet gone but already gone
weeps on the couch with a warm budweiser
and a red haired boy next to her draws
a door another door any
door

shame dream 3

i put my son to sleep on a sheet of white
in a field while we eat and drink
and soon all the music piles trash on top
of trash and people step over people

cities of garbage proliferate
all over the earth and white paper
and boxes and sun-bleached blankets
clump into hills and my son

my son where is my son?
he is not awake? i drop my cup
and begin digging through each body
of refuse like i am scratching through

my own cavities but nothing is there
i find a white sheet with a dead cabbage
and half a hamburger i find a dead bat
i find dusty toys i lost as a child

i can't find him he is gone my throat
is lost my hands are inside my
chest my son is gone and when
i wake i am still clutching

the sheets

shame dream 4

back in college but late for class
the dorm too far away to walk and the road
a sand hill caving in so i ride with a group
of women who are studying to be midwives
i am late into the lecture hall and i drop my books
so loudly the lecturer who had been extoling the bravery
of midwives (am i studying to be a midwife?
do they allow men?) rushes over to humiliate me
with a smile and all the sudden she is a man

everyone is male with beards and my books
and lunch and porno mags with pictures
of naked men drape across my lap
(i am not gay what are these doing here?)
i don't look up but place everything
back in my wet
backpack

shame dream 5

i try to pick up the boy but he is me
and my arms are disaster and coal

and the ocean burns us as it
rolls in

the rain on august 6ᵗʰ doesn't mean anything

but it does the rain means
i don't need to drink

it means i don't have to seek
revenge

my friend at work says *god puts certain
people on this earth to test you*

and even in the burnt-lawn swelter
i will not lash out

but explain why i deserve whatever
every creature earns

by just walking on this earth a lightly
falling prayer in sheets of grace

which makes each being capacious
in their burgeoning

i don't know why i have to explain
that i too am here

not a thin hologram in an iniquitous
tragedy feet on dry river rock

but a thing such as grass where holes
can be watered and made verdant

such a thing as a treefrog hiding
in this garden of the knowledge of good and evil

waiting for some word to quench
my skin

each

word sticks a needle
in a silver moth—

wings still thrashing
against the paper

morning prayer to be recited waist deep in the sulfurous rubble of sodom and gomorrah

give the sun a chance to rise
out of the ashes

give each hollow bone
a vacation from howling

give the dry places in between
a way to bathe without list or task

give the sex a flood of
permission

give those lonely people inside
a lullaby and a lemonade

give those policemen in the brows
acupuncture and plate of sleep

give to the giver because the office is empty
and none of the cards have been signed

give to the underwater sisters and brothers
a parcel of air there is a whole sky full

give god a lament
and a broken toy

sing the sun up out
of the ashes

as long as there is breath there can be song
as long as there is breath there can be song

prayer in endless pain and endless burning

god will still be with you if you hurt
even more so even through the fire

god will still ease whatever can be
eased

as we learn to walk with burns
with courage god will come to you

as family as small tasks in the
morning

as a dish of empathy before
sleep

prayer for harpies' teeth and harpies' tongues

i can't remember everyone who told me i was worthless
but i know exactly who yelled at me for whatever reason

(i scream at my children sometimes / i am a devil / my
father taught me to scream / he is dead too young
because the rage perverted his marrow)

i know every person has these memories boxed and taped
in the intercranial space fomenting like spiderwombs

i can't write this correctly because of the anger spitting
out of god's wounds of each innocent pair of hands
deskinned by fear

by people who don't love themselves enough
(so easy to say / so easy to say)

by people who have no skin because they never realized
they deserve to grow it back

by people who are jealous or careful of each sharp fang
lining their milky mouths

(i am not innocent / i am in the whirlpool of serpents
with half of my body flayed)

i want all of these grafts to bud along a glowing edge—
anemone pulp and fleshgill

if god was a medicine / if love was easy / if words
did not hurt

we could be chrome and steam and hands melting butter

we could answer with yes with a silent silver hum
our mercury a shield inside a sleep

a holding of all the light
that was stolen

i will need to

learn the language of spiders

stop fearing my son will die
in his sleep

keep the wide sky and all the water
in my cracked chest

be kind when i am scared my lord
be kind when i am angry

quiet the shaking in all phases of the
vengeful moon

the apocalypse is how i bite off
my family's fingers as i smile and cough

if i can't master myself the world is lost—
a turtle mauled by time by each clicking ant

if i can't still this howling the spiders
will try to silence me in my bed

both light and dark
have their webs

i will try to talk them out of it
i will speak through the vents

i will need to
learn the language of spiders

tell them i am dry already
tell them i am dry

the first cold morning of late summer

shears off more space to breathe
clears branches bronchioles

with a merciful
dark

the light is still green

but i draw the hanged man
from the deck

whether or not i heed the signs
doesn't mean that god isn't keeping score

of the lies of the unpunished laughter
between sleeping

there are no words to fill
the blank

but i still write—look
the void fleshed and feathered!

spells to retain each afternoon
in stubborn catalogues of smoke

but my garden will still turn yellow
in november

my children will still grow past the point
where i can carry them

i will still feel longing for losing
what i think i don't have

what i think i can't hold
i will still cry when i look back at what i believe

were these glorious teeth-lined grins and growls
these barely survivable weeks

i better enjoy it
i guess—

the gasping and going back
under

i need a plot

of dandelion bindweed thistle
red clover loosestrife moss
i need hydra-necks of blackberry
and english ivy springing
heavenward

nourish it with pooled blood
with epinephrine with insomnia's
lymph with sinkbowl semen
with skin and skin and skin
and prayers for revenge

i need for the things i always
pull out to flourish
somewhere i need to
keep the darkness
fed

beneath every word i utter

there is a quieter voice
also speaking—

whispering at the holy ghost
cursing into the hole

between us

there are two worlds

one manifest—stoplights flags words
and jails on the vast fir-rooted earth
and each heavy tear of the brackish flood

one unmanifest—in the hollow of things
where crows and snow crabs and harvestmen
spiders stretch through

(children can see it before they are taught
they cannot / most of us won't know it until
the line on the monitor rests)

but sometimes when the afternoon light slants
over the cedars—the golden ghost reaches
out to be witnessed—

a testament to the jeweled ether inside mass
a promise that each unwrapping is a release—
each death a dive back in

what if

instead of my face
pictured on my id badge

it was my transparent feet
and everyone could see what i had to walk

through to get here—a map of clouded bruises
and pale suns rising up the arches?

what if it was my mirrored hands
of spot and pearl reflecting all

whom i have touched—a betrayal
a prayer?

what if it was my heart—
tired meat-hollow laboring through

crystal ribs—trying to hold it all in
while spitting?

some

hope for the morning
when there aren't any prayers big enough

to stop love from peeling off like paint
to protect my children from excoriation

i guess i should just drink this coffee
take a photo of the snow-skinned roses

in the fascia-blue air
i guess i should forgive god

but not myself
not yet

accordion mirrors

when the zucchini bread rises
and the spaghetti sauce pops and the counters
have been wiped and the clothes have been nestled
when the sweeping is swept and the house is hot
and the baby is cribbed with 30 more minutes
of projected nap what do i do but try to make
words hum?

to give meaning to the rock rolling and the spill
mopping? to hold these moments of rest like sacred
tokens? to tap a few shapes on a screen? to place
a burnt card back into the deck? i don't know
what to do with myself nowadays because my image
is parceled out—the young man a folded photo
the writer a mimic

the husband an inhabited bed
the cynic and the monk a dirty story
but i'll be glad to see my daughter and wife
when they return i'll be elated when my son
wakes the me lifting him the father
i wish i truly was

the monk or the cynic?

fill my hands with unseen light
empty my light with unseen hands

why is this body always thirsty
for a thing it cannot define?

my daughter is scared of goodwill

says the objects carry spirits of the owners
just the dust and the ghosts of too many people
she refuses to go in

i think of dead men's loafers twitching to walk
a painting of an ocean damaged by decades of light
a toy fire engine that no longer wails

maybe she is right maybe if i listen
i will hear years of arguments smoking the mirrors
i will taste all the voices boxed forgotten

sold

résumé

i bring back ashes
from the obsidian
river

god of late summer rain

my son's shoes wet
after he kicks off the blanket

i repeat *rain rain* to him
in the stroller

his hand reaching out
touching grace

on its way down

prayer for an anxious father

hold god
like a sleeping child

there is nothing
in my hands

but joyful
weeping

i don't know why

i wake 10 minutes before
my alarm

do i stretch up a tentacle
to eye the clock?

and does the rest of me remain
invertebrate in the black canticle

even after i rise?
even after i reskin all of these

words?

i think i can create

a field of rain-fed wildflowers
from memory from symbols splashed on a screen

i attempt it tenderly with a borrowed god
my empty hands opening closing on each key

but when i listen to coltrane's *my favorite things*
i know i fail

i hear the sky's circus bloom
and the dna gleams up my spine

through the pollen of every flower
in every field—a hollow-thick misery —

a lymph a falling a prayer—
recklessly weightless with each

step

giving the ego a poetry award

is like applauding the baton
after the woodwind brass and strings
have lifted the blood to the stars

or like praising a broken shell
for the oeuvre of the pacific's
advancing roar

some days i can't believe

this life is possible—
these conduits of salt and bile

reaching up to an electric coil
held up by calcified long-feathers

these digits twitch at my command
this voice swells out of air

caught between terror and wonder
some days i can't believe

we replicate by seed and egg
arching backs and release

beings who will again lift out
of this swirling dust and question

how is this formed to flourish?
with what magic is this conjured?

with what clouds can we translate
the stretch and break? the concurrence?

with who's embrace is this made
survivable?

the war is to

stay in the body when anxiety
splits the glass

i usually find myself coiled in a closet
behind burnt mothwings

today the september blue lifts all life
silk-lipped before the frost

allows fibonacci intercostals to unspool
invites my ghost to sweep through

this interior still in embers
my ether eyes spill into these glassy orbs

just in time to let the purple flame
of asters in

most times

i don't like to talk
but float in god's aqueous humor

my fingers clearing the fog
off the lens

some mornings

i am the broken
appliance on the sidewalk

the free sign detached
all my gears gaping

at the rust of
god

walking with my wife at work

we are 15 years younger!
so light the rain

does not hit
us

i used to take benadryl

when i couldn't sleep
i have since found that my heart

recharges too long between q and t
and antihistamines can crayon

my rhythm vvvvvvv across the screen
and flap my ventricles like a sail

now when sleep does not take me
i wait and wait and wait

for my heart to catch up
for my mind to cartoon itself

into nothing

as i child

i swallowed my voice
while my parents screamed

my glottal pit has since blistered —
mirroring the inside of pearls

these words i write
are still silent

i can pretend i am speaking
but really i am still at the top

of the stairs waiting
for the fight

to end

sometimes i wonder

which of my classmates have died
i know a few—an estranged best friend

an ex-girlfriend (sometimes i try to speak
to them in the afternoon lull)

then i feel like i know the others
who have gone because i can't

picture their faces as still intact
but clayrubbed with flashes of wing

i wonder if anyone suspects i am dead
(i wonder if i do) sometimes my body

doesn't feel attached sometimes i can
come and go

it doesn't scare me like it did as a child
to slip into the lobby during the feature

hear the silver chatter of the ushers
feel them guide me back to my seat

with a pull on my collarbone
hear them tell me *stay in your body*

hear them say *play your role*
and pretend you never saw us

feel them stare at me
as i rustle in my skin

as i rock him i begin to see

a squadron of seabirds fly above
a fleet of fish swim below

the birds are hopes
the fish are fears

my son is asleep
as they encircle him

he stands on an island as small
as a body he stands and watches

each fish become a bird
each bird become a fish

where ocean and sky
swell together

as a breath

when i finally don't feel anxiety

i can listen to the quiet clicks
of the hummingbirds in the cedar

while watching my son pull carrots
soil-bathed from the garden

i can hear my wife on the porch
feel the warmth of just sipping her in

i can eat and taste and cook corn soup
and pasta and pull weeds and never dread

the oncoming demons the invisible takers
i can paint with my daughter

serene moonscapes inside with disembodied
eyes and fishtails and toothed eels

there are things growing again in the painting
among the nerves strung on stained shards

she says *i don't think much when i paint*
i just let it come out

thank god it is not hereditary—
the meat-jawed cartoons or the clenching

or at least she has learned to paint them
in red streaks over distant hills

in a black sky spun with familiar
ghosts

whiskey is a horrible anti-anxiety medicine and why i don't drink anymore

after my first drink
100 televisions unplug

but at 3 am 1000 televisions wake me
along with a howling gibbon

the next day another drink maybe 2 or 3 —
relative quiet except anger

subtle at first as i spit at my family
but i really spit at god at the falling floor

at myself as a drop away
why am i angry if i am actually

scared the fear will never stop?
i can't unplug this unless

i find the boy shaking
some round holes in his thorax

he says *don't help me i can do this*
myself i am not dissolving

i am not crying
but i pull him into some light

i make by holding my chest and my testicles

53

and asking god (the god with spit

on his face) to heal me and he
does but so slowly

the holes still weep
mercury

as i pray

why i write all these poems

i am here to burn the pith
out of every spruce

my body a hollow
inhabited by flying things

i give each colony of bees a hole
i open my tongue to termites

(are these my wings i have
swallowed?)

and every so often
the light shines down my throat

glissading off each charcoaled cell
and i fill with what i have lost

(or have i gained god?)
some flame which still warms

me on its way
through

poetry as a type of monkhood

sometimes people give me respect for my poems
treat me like i am something special

but this always makes me feel uncomfortable
in this vow i have taken there is no special

only listening
only skinless in the cereal aisle

only coelacanth spleens from the bottom of trenches
only an ache like splintering femurs

only silence in the dark five years old
heart blistering in the ears

only an unhealthy longing for a pretend god
only an envelope on a web

only an opal
only

awake at 4 am for no reason i think about

how spices blown on a person's face
or deliberately rubbed silver-fingered
through the hair could alter
one's dreams:

cacao- the darkness within the body
bleeds and clots and sweetens
cilantro- the tortillas are burning
and the flesh is delicious

cinnamon- moab july dust
the fire ants dance up the arches
clove- the smoke pops alveoli
in the alley of the blacklights

cumin- the feet have become
the earth the arroyo breathes
mint- the first frost of october
brocades the sage

sage- sleeps through winter
white shouldered with words
salt- scrapes the eyes along
the openings of wounds

salt- brings the fish to the throat
delivers the moon
salt- begs to stop
crying

thyme- falls off and leaves
tiny bones in the sky

i try to take part of me away

i have tried drinking
but that just makes that part angry

i exercise hard enough to force it to gasp
and struggle and sleep for a day or so

but it still awakens at 3 am—
a dread in the breath

each inhalation a cragged mountain
each pulse a flood of wasps

maybe 20,000 years ago these genetics
saved my family from a night attack

when a twig broke under a foot
of a mammalian intruder

and all the flame of all the stars
opened these eyes

and i tore tooth and tendon
with these hands these trembling hands

still anointed with
blood

shame dream 6

i sip the tepid beer
on the table because

the others are doing that but
i don't know how they swallow

because they don't have
mouths

then i realize i have to begin
my sober date again today

when i look up
i am in a stomach

the fundal folds glisten
in the dim light

and the fritos on the table
taste like the f

i got on the math test
in third grade

i want a new holy book

something brief and instructive and full
of photographs and illustrations like a zine
love being the glue on the binder the parables
morphing to each's need or cultural reference
or it could be generic like: *love yourself as god*
loves you and love others with that glow
the afterlife could be handled with:
before and after this body you were light
and will be again (and still are)
all the evils of the world could be
under the heading of *free will poorly used*
with a collage of murder and rape
and deceit and abuse and willful ignorance
war would have its own page: *the rich profit*
by convincing people to kill one another is all it would say
nutrition and exercise would read:
if you wish your body to be here longer
but illness and death with:
your body is not perfect and it will break
from time to time until it stops for good and you return
grief with: *let yourself feel the loss*
and the moon phase through the darkness
the world with: *the glory is in every leaf stone and beast*
sex with: *enjoy your body but share it only with mutual love*
and gentleness (unless you both are kinky)
and for the hole in the pit of the aura:
your demons are angels screaming at you to release
the ropes around your neck
for false advertising and politics

there would be an ad with a doctor smoking
pall malls on his desk a photo of nixon grinning:
not all that is written or shown is true
at the end there would be pages to be written on
opposite pages with mirrors
there will be a page for every day
of the rest of your life
just don't count the pages
that would be cheating

shame dream 7

another dream about teaching
and again i am talking and students
just get up and walk out of the door

somewhere i realize i don't teach anymore
so i just keep reading from the book
hiroshima by hersey as the kids disappear

at least i think they were not vaporized
by a thermonuclear bomb and least i think
they were not shot at least i think they can

decide what to do because they are not held
in my failed sepia classroom my fear of
losing all of them to boredom such a relief

so much better than losing them to a
broken sky a hot metal pit a permanent
sleep

i weep when i write

don't fucking ask me why
maybe i open so much

that i am scared of myself
naked in the hostile air

plus i have to give you something
from inside the broken costumes

inside the monkey statue
inside the half-formed meatmask

inside the red milk falling into light
i remember now

the light is what i am supposed
to bring you

but when i hold it out it is full of ants
and ruptures

and i have to wash my hands
again

one of these days i will stop
trying and stay immaculate

only on the outside

the fortune cookie

inside my chest can only be
seen when the tide is receding

when the sun slants through
the ribslats

inside is a blank wing
which does not know it is a wing

it is not a fortune cookie
but a blood-valved clamshell

screaming and drinking
as a heart does

quietly
pretending to be full

but if there was a fortune cookie

in my chest what would be written
on the wet confetti inside?

there are no words which can take
the place of love

the clear answer

when i ask the ether
(or the god tangled in my veins)

why i carry so much anxiety
why i flash open this fetid

phosphorus and splay
woundlipped

is:
so you remember how to heal

i don't want to be the dolphin

who does backflips for baitfish
my whole life

twisting my spine for praise
or at least i want to feel the thrust

of my muscle through the water
enjoy the lift and rotation

of flight—out of the enclosure
for a few seconds the cement

now miles of pacific
breath

to read when i am anxious

1. you will get through this you have always
survived and flourished even if not overtly

2. the pain is temporary and the temporary is a low
pressure from the ocean drenching the chaparral

3. breathing can open something like god
to hang the openings on

4. love is the only substance and fear is also love
with fingers gripping into the fabric and tearing

5. forgive your mind for its traffic and poor merging
(sometimes a thumbs up works better than the bird)

6. forgive the heart for its galloping through
the wind-wrestled smalltalk or the noisy dark

7. know that water is always water
regardless of boiling or crystal lock

8. if you smile and shine a prayer
on your quivering body it will also glow

9. the glow means there is a tree growing
through your solarplexis into both poles

10. the glow means you will rest even if bisected
the glow means the divine is a tongue

11. the glow means the divide is divine

otosclerosis and mandibular tori

are the scientific names for abnormal
bone growth in the ear canal and under the tongue

one has been drilled out of my auditory meatus
while i was asleep

the other has erected a row of bone hotels
nestling my lower teeth

why is my skull trying to grow over its openings?
for safety? for a muffled mouthless bliss?

somewhere in me there is a need to cover
no matter what speech or song is lost

i should be thankful that my frontal and zygomatic
arches have not yet quested to close

against the light

anxiety (as an artist)

consists of a pith-lipped narrator
(who is not you nor me nor god)

concocting fictional futures
and each scene erases

present tense in
a paroxysm

of ink

walking in the late october gusts

the oak leaves braille across the path
in front of me and for a second

i fear they will tear through
my legs if i go forward

and i think when
did i get so

fragile?

i have said it before

but those squirrels are up to something
every october they know that we are weak

and they chatter and mock us
and store our hopes

and our light
in secret holes

the crows know too
they have tried for millennia

to teach us how to exchange our bodies
for charcoal and moonspit when the doors

are still visible before the dark closes
in around our throats

but we have never listened but string
our false suns around our homes

like a mistranslated spell
and sing songs of a man

who brought the light to us
and was murdered for it

or songs of light which endured
eight days on one day's oil

as if this could bring a submerged star
back to this northern sky

the crows are in the water under and through
as they dance between doorways

bringing the light through in swaths of
wingbeat and caterwaul

the squirrels dig their way there
as we look up impuissant

and plead with a blank
dark heaven

some days the restaurant of life

is filled with streetwater
so my socks weep dyspepsic

and the table in the back
near the executioner and the priest

is the only one open
and is still a 45 minute wait

the menu is greasy with toddler snot
and the only entrée is a whale amygdala

stuffed with worry and cardamom
during the meal several cats swim over

and piss on the chair next to mine
and the waiter with scorpion elbows

keeps filling up my collar with chamomile tea
and attaching my eeg leads to the leafblower

when it is time to leave my family
has always been here but they loved

the meal they are wondering
what is wrong with me

they want to come back here
tomorrow

i want to send a letter

"We all got holes to fill
them holes are all that's real"
                    -Townes Van Zandt

i want to send a letter
to my children no i want to show

them by my actions and comport
that love fills all the holes

that love prevents falls from hurting
and bones from snapping

and trust from lying
and hearts from infarcting

and people and cats from dying
that love can solve everything

if radiated from an open chest
like a broken sprinkler

no

when i send the letter it will say:

love is more real than pain

love created everything
is everything

go back to love when you are lost,
my children

the graffiti on the path

painted with purple letters
reads *you got this!*

i think:
you don't know me

you don't know what part
of this park i already lift

and carry you don't know how
loving makes each step

ache but also float
the far banks of the puget sound

peel up and levitate as i pray
for health for the safety of cars

and planes and viruses
for my two children and my wife

to be whole and settled during
this contretemps of gravity

i say thank you to the buoyant
entity who wrote this message

on my path and are you still
alive i want to know

are you still
alive?

it has always eluded me how god

like a multidimensional santa claus
keeps track of karma and balance

what is given what is taken
in a penumbra of shadow and law

but why did i ever believe
that this world is just?

when has it been just to me?
in the middle of this poem

our furnace stopped working
and it is getting down to 37 tonight

we were able to start the gas fireplace
at least and put the space heater

in the baby's room while he sleeps
we compensate and bargain

while god takes and gives each degree
in this fragile peace between

birth and death

ghostly fall light

on the sage
no one cares

about the glow
without its antithesis

no one measures brightness
against a glare

and no one can see through
death without a silver

voice from the other
shore

sonnet

-after Diane Seuss

it was supposed to be easier than this
after the flood but my brain still looks
like an electrician's garage and i don't
want to scare you mythically but my snakehair
snaps back and i still can't sleep with these
movements crowding the rain like iambs
i have to get up and type this into the fossil
record before this extinction event slips
back into the bedrock but what did i gain
eyes can't even look at myself in a mirror
for fear of stoning? that wasn't a question
for the warehouse rats chewing on the wires
it wasn't a saved poem it doesn't help
anyone i can't turn this thing off anyhow

god is a used car

if i break my key off
in the door
who do i ask
to let me
in?

when i cradle him god cradles me

when i put him to sleep i try to rub his head
and his back to teach him that tenderness
is possible that the sirens and hungers
have soft hands that at least now
he can believe this so that even
after the stage combusts and
falls he will grip his first role
this single word unmasked
in its veined pouch and
he will believe it will be
enough and he will
stand and grin
into the
dark

dear scott

i am writing this to you knowing that the parts
of you hooked to the worry-talons may be sheared
off by the medicine you are going to start

i hope it does not tear too much of the skin
around the amygdala up through the hypothalamus
reaching up through a fountain of epinephrine

they say there could be a removal of the cock
and balls and the higher joys with the extrication
of the many-mouthed demons

we could see the suffering artist replaced by a
functioning slab of sores healing in a gel
of serotonin and dental office flute music

i hope we will still be in touch through the curtain
of medium grey soap i hope when you laugh
you will feel it in the spirals of each mitochondria

i hope when you cry you will remember how
to stop please promise me if it takes too much
from you please spill the pills in the whale's

maw please come back into the shiny pain
with new wounds please remember all of us
speaking at once like a substitute classroom

please say a prayer for us each time you swallow
the poison please walk out of this
bombshelter and never come back

when i was still listening

to the bastard voice teeth-clamped
on my larynx like a lamprey

i didn't think i deserved
to dance any more

i took the medicine now i no longer
hear any of my most intimate parasites

now i can listen to myself—
a mirror with water limbs

i am still here i have been patiently
painting the walls with moon-semen

drafting maps for unwalling the air
between breaths

winging new physics equations
for owl-whisked silence

through this forest of frozen-necked
nerves which now

has just become people
with round teeth with lips

which kiss which spit laughter
with warm wet mouths

which welcome me back
into this flesh

About the Poet

Scott Ferry helps our Veterans heal as a RN in the Seattle area. In former lives he taught high school, managed aquatic centers, and practiced acupuncture. He has four books of poetry: The only thing that makes sense is to  grow (Moon Tide, 2019), Mr. Rogers kills fruit flies (Main St. Rag, 2020), These Hands of Myrrh (Kelsay Books, 2021), and Sea of Marrow (Ethel Press, 2021). He has another book upcoming in 2022: fishmirror from Alien Buddha Press.

Made in the USA
Middletown, DE
16 January 2022

58851069R00050